◇TELL ME ABOUT◇

BUILDINGS BRIDGES & TUNNELS

SERIES EDITOR: JACKIE GAFF

Kingfisher Books

Series designer: Terry Woodley
Author: Jackie Gaff
Consultant: Ralph Mills
Contributors: Angela Royston, Louise Pritchard
Designer: David West Children's Book Design
Illustrators: David Etchell (pp. 10–11, 24–5, 32–3);
Micheal Fisher (pp. 2–3, 12–19, 22–3, 28–9); Kevin
Madison (pp. 8–9, 26–7, 36–7); Alex Pang (pp. 1, 30–1);
Sebastien Quigley (pp. 34–5, 38); Ross Watton (pp. 6–7);
Steve Weston (pp. 4–5, 20–1, 39).
Cover illustration: Chris Forsey

Kingfisher Books, Grisewood & Dempsey Ltd, Elsley
House, 24–30 Great Titchfield Street, London W1P 7AD

First published in 1991 by Kingfisher Books
Copyright © Grisewood & Dempsey Ltd 1991

BRITISH LIBRARY CATALOGUING IN PUBLICATION DATA
Buildings, bridges & tunnels.
    1. Buildings
    I. Gaff, Jackie   11. Series
    690

ISBN 0 86272 559 3
Phototypeset by Southern Positives and Negatives
(SPAN), Lingfield, Surrey. Printed in Spain.

Contents

Why are buildings important?

Thousands of years ago, when people first started to build things, they used tree branches and animal skins to make huts to shelter them from harsh weather. Nowadays we build homes in all sorts of shapes and sizes, from towering blocks of flats to single-storey cottages and bungalows. But big or small, these buildings are still important for the shelter and protection they give us.

The earliest buildings were homes, but we now construct all sorts of different buildings and use them in many different ways.

Housing estates and blocks of flats are places built for people to live in.

Buildings where people go to relax and spend their free time include cinemas, theatres and sports stadiums.

? DO YOU KNOW

Religious buildings such as churches and mosques are among the most beautiful and magnificent structures in the world. One of the world's largest churches is St Peter's in Rome, Italy. It's nearly 210 metres long and about 137 metres across at its widest point. There's room for more than 50,000 people inside.

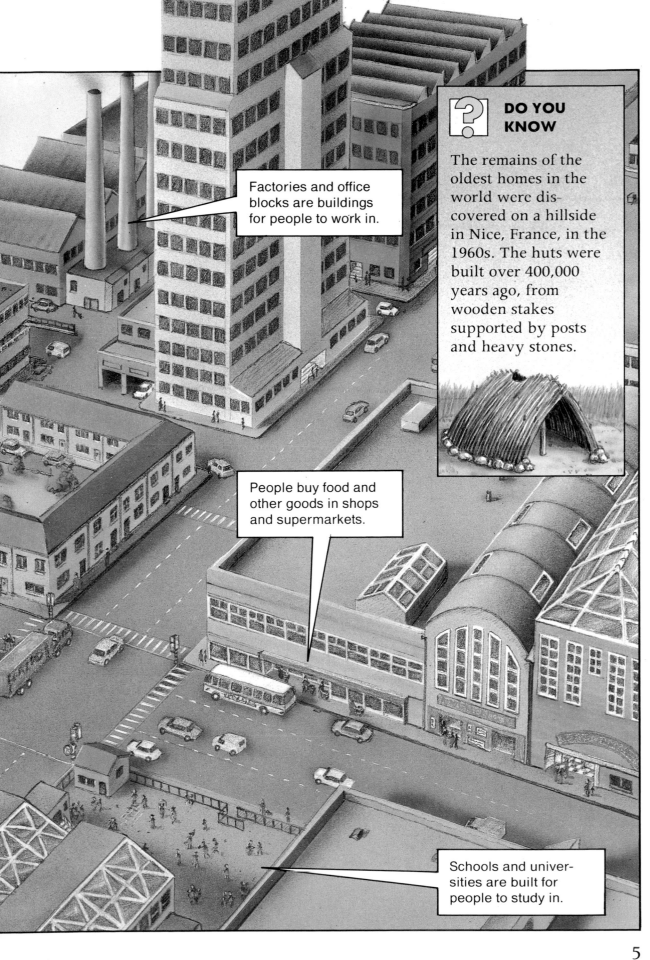

Factories and office blocks are buildings for people to work in.

DO YOU KNOW

The remains of the oldest homes in the world were discovered on a hillside in Nice, France, in the 1960s. The huts were built over 400,000 years ago, from wooden stakes supported by posts and heavy stones.

People buy food and other goods in shops and supermarkets.

Schools and universities are built for people to study in.

How are houses built?

Houses have to be designed and planned before building work begins, and architects are the people whose job it is to do this. The builders use the architect's plans as a guide while they are working on the house.

All modern buildings have foundations. These provide a firm base for the frame of the building, and they stop heavy structures from sinking into soft ground.

The foundation trenches are filled with concrete, which sets hard to make a firm base for the house.

The house site is measured out and marked with posts and string.

Trenches are dug for foundations, and to take water pipes and electricity cables.

DESIGN A HOUSE

This is what an architect's plans are like – they show what the house will look like, inside and out. Use the plans as a model for designing a house of your own. How many rooms would you need? What would you use them for? Don't forget to put in windows, doors and stairs!

FRONT   SIDE

DOWNSTAIRS   UPSTAIRS

Stairs   Hall   Kitchen   Dining-room   Living-room

Bath-room   Bedroom   Bed   Bedroom

Door   Window

Carpenters and joiners fit doors and windows, as well as laying floorboards and building the frame for the roof.

Bricklayers build walls on the foundations – concrete blocks are used inside, bricks outside.

Plumbers fit pipes to carry water around the house. They also put in sinks and baths, and the central heating system.

Electricians put in wires and cables to carry the electricity. They fit lights, plugs and switches.

BUILDING FACTS

● Concrete is a very hard building material which is sometimes used instead of bricks or stone, as well as for foundations. It's made by mixing sand, small stones, cement and water – it sets like rock when dry.

● Bricks are made by baking clay at very high temperatures.

● Cement is made by mixing and burning clay and chalk, then grinding them into a fine powder. It's used in concrete and mortar.

● Mortar is used in wall-building to stick bricks and stones together. It's a gritty paste which dries hard. It's made by mixing sand, cement and water.

7

Which are the largest houses?

The largest houses in the world are palaces, where rulers such as kings and queens live. One of the world's largest private houses is Biltmore House in North Carolina, USA. It has more than 250 rooms, including 32 guest bedrooms and its own gymnasium, swimming pool and bowling alley!

Biltmore House was built for George W. Vanderbilt in 1890–95, in the style of 16th-century French châteaux, or castles. The Vanderbilt family no longer lives there, and the house and its beautiful gardens are open for the public to visit.

 HOUSE FACTS

• A fisherman's cottage in Conwy, North Wales, is one of the world's smallest houses. It's less than 2 metres wide and just over 3 metres high. Inside it only has a staircase and two tiny rooms – most adults wouldn't be able to stand up straight in them!

FISHERMAN'S COTTAGE, CONWY

• There are many large palaces throughout the world, but few are still lived in as homes. The largest palace which is still a home is that of the Sultan of Brunei, a tiny country in South-East Asia. It has more than 1780 rooms and about 250 toilets!

Which are the tallest buildings?

The tallest buildings in the world are skyscrapers, and the world's tallest skyscraper is the Sears Tower in Chicago, USA. This gigantic building is 110 storeys high and soars 443 metres above street level – that's almost half a kilometre! It has 16,000 windows and more than 100 lifts.

1 Chrysler Building (319 metres high), New York, USA, 1930.

2 Empire State Building (381 metres high), New York, 1931

3 World Trade Center (twin towers, 412 metres high), New York, 1973.

4 Sears Tower (443 metres high), Chicago, USA, 1974.

 DO YOU KNOW

The largest city in the USA, New York City, has more skyscrapers than anywhere else in the world. Most of them are on the island of Manhattan.

WIND TESTING

Did you know that tall buildings are designed to sway in high winds so that they don't shake themselves to pieces and fall down?

To see how wind affects tall buildings, make a long tube out of thin card and tape its base to a table. Then use a hair dryer to blow 'wind' at your tower.

How are skyscrapers built?

Skyscrapers are very heavy because they are so tall. This means that they need firm foundations to support their weight and a strong framework to hold them together. The framework of most skyscrapers is made from long metal beams called girders. The floors and walls are supported by the framework and can be added as each storey is completed.

PULLEY POWER

1 Cranes use pulleys to help them lift. Ask an adult to help you make one from wire and cotton reels.

2 Load a toy bucket with heavy objects and tie a piece of cord to its handle. Lift the bucket by the cord. Now thread the cord around your pulley. Is the bucket easier to lift now?

Pulley

Workers wear hard hats to protect their heads, and safety straps in case they fall.

A goods lift carries materials, tools and workers up and down.

Ready-made glass or metal panels called cladding are used for the outside walls. They are lifted into position by cranes.

Long metal beams called girders are bolted together to make the framework.

Floors are made by pouring concrete on to a metal or temporary wooden framework. Sometimes ready-made concrete slabs are used instead.

Water, electricity and air-conditioning pipes are fitted in the spaces between the floors and the ceilings below.

FOUNDATION FACTS

Piles

• The foundations for most skyscrapers have long 'legs' called piles. They work rather like tree roots, anchoring the skyscraper and supporting its weight.

Drill

• Piles are sometimes made on site. Deep holes are drilled in the ground and lined with metal girders or rods. The holes are then filled with concrete.

• Sometimes piles are made in a factory and brought to the site. They are hammered into the ground bit by bit using a pile-driver – a weight lifted and dropped by a crane.

What were the Seven Wonders?

The Seven Wonders of the World were some of the most spectacular structures of ancient times. They were described over 2000 years ago, by a Greek writer called Antipater of Sidon. Over the centuries, some of the Seven Wonders collapsed and fell into ruin. Others were destroyed by fires or earthquakes. Only the pyramids at Giza are still standing today.

1 The Giza pyramids were built about 4500 years ago. They are the oldest of the Seven Wonders (the others were built 2500–2000 years ago), the only ones still standing.

DO YOU KNOW

The pyramids of Egypt were built as tombs for pharaohs, or kings.

Pharaoh's tomb

The largest, the Great Pyramid at Giza, was over 146 metres high and took thousands of workers more than 30 years to build. Over 2 million blocks of stone had to be cut and hauled into place by hand. People think that today it would take at least 400 workers using modern equipment more than five years to build it.

2 The greenery and flowers of the Hanging Gardens of Babylon were particularly amazing because they were created in the middle of the desert.

3 The Temple of Artemis at Ephesus was one of the largest temples of ancient times. Its columns were over six times the height of a man.

4 The Colossus of Rhodes was a huge bronze statue of the Greek sun god Helios. It was destroyed by an earthquake less than 60 years after it was completed.

5 The tomb at Halicarnassus was built for a ruler called Mausolus. It was over 40 metres high – so big that all large tombs were called mausoleums after it.

GREECE

3

7

4

5

Mediterranean Sea

2

6

EGYPT

1

MODERN WONDERS

Amazing and beautiful buildings are still being constructed all over the world. Which ones would you choose to put in a modern list of the Seven Wonders of the World?

Would you include Australia's Sydney Opera House, for example – its extraordinary roof makes it look like a ship in full sail!

6 The Lighthouse at Alexandria was more than 120 metres high, and the fire burning at its top could be seen by ships many kilometres out to sea.

7 The Statue of Zeus (the king of the Greek gods) at Olympia was made of gold and ivory and inset with precious stones.

How long is the Great Wall of China?

At nearly 3500 km long – nearly five times the distance between London and Paris – the Great Wall of China is the largest structure ever built. It was begun over 2200 years ago, during the rule of the emperor Shi Huangdi, as a defence against fierce tribes which were trying to invade China from the north.

? DO YOU KNOW

The Great Wall of China is the only structure built by people which can be seen from the Moon.

The Great Wall winds across the mountains and valleys of northern China for nearly 3500 km. It has more than 2850 km of additional, branching walls.

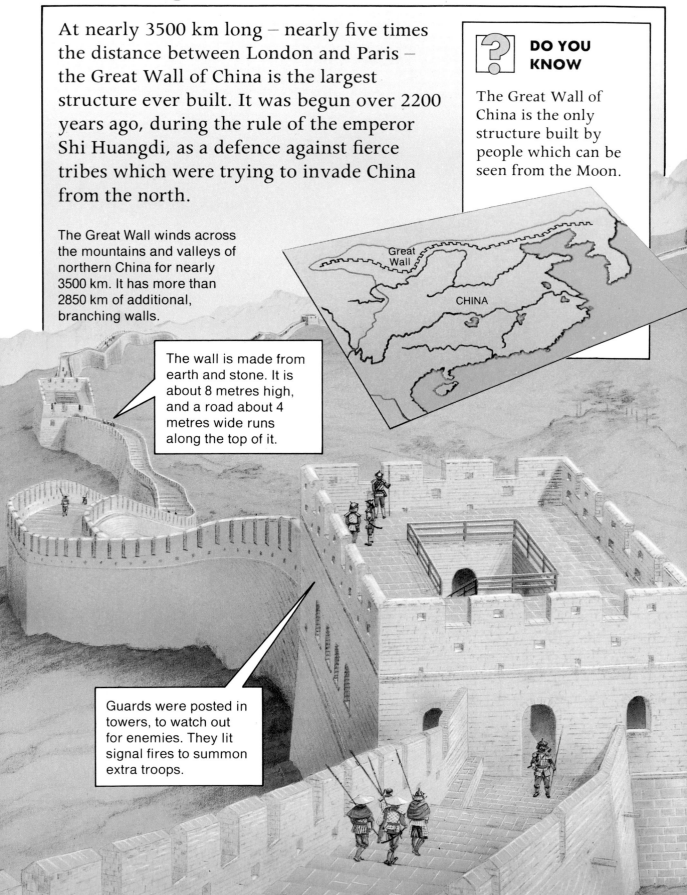

Great Wall

CHINA

The wall is made from earth and stone. It is about 8 metres high, and a road about 4 metres wide runs along the top of it.

Guards were posted in towers, to watch out for enemies. They lit signal fires to summon extra troops.

Who built the Parthenon?

The Parthenon was built by the Ancient Greeks over 2300 years ago, as a temple for the goddess Athena. Its ruins are still standing today, on a hill called the Acropolis in the Greek city of Athens.

The Ancient Greeks used rows of thick stone pillars called columns to support beams and roofs.

Beam

Columns

Who built the Colosseum?

The Colosseum is in Rome, the capital city of Italy. It was built by the Romans nearly 2000 years ago, as a giant sports arena.

Romans went to the Colosseum to see men called gladiators fighting each other. Gladiators also fought wild animals such as lions.

DO YOU KNOW

The Romans were able to construct bigger and stronger buildings than the Ancient Greeks because they learnt how to use arches – these can carry more weight than columns and beams.

Arches

15

How were castles built?

European kings and lords began building stone castles about 1000 years ago, to protect themselves and their lands from enemies. Because castles were designed to resist enemy attack, they had very high thick walls – up to 12 times the height of a man and 4 to 6 metres thick.

Workers had simple tools in those days, so castle-building took a long time. Around 1000 people would have worked for as long as ten years building a medium-sized castle.

Roofs were often covered with tiles made from wood or thin stone.

Only the outside of the walls were stone. The middle was made of rubble set with mortar.

Wooden scaffolding was built as the walls grew higher. Heavy loads were dragged up ramps or hoisted up on ropes and pulleys.

Workers used picks and shovels to dig trenches for foundations. These were filled with rubble and set with mortar.

CASTLE FACTS

● The largest castle in the world that people still live in is Windsor Castle, which belongs to the British royal family. It covers roughly the same area as 12.5 football pitches!

● The Kremlin, in Moscow in the USSR, was built over 500 years ago for the Russian tsars, or kings. It has 20 towers and its pink walls rise to over 18 metres.

● Castles weren't just built in Europe. Japanese lords began building stone castles about 450 years ago, for example. The walls of their castles often sloped inwards.

Stairs were made from shaped pieces of stone. Each step was supported by the one below.

The heaviest loads were lifted by wooden cranes. A man walked inside a wheel, to make it wind in a rope as it turned.

Why does the Tower of Pisa lean?

This famous Italian building started tilting to one side as soon as it first three storeys were completed. Its foundations aren't strong enough to support its weight, and it started leaning as it began sinking into the soft ground beneath it.

The tower was built in 1173–1372. It is still tilting, at a rate of about 1.25 mm a year. Its top is now nearly 5 metres to one side of its base.

? DO YOU KNOW

The Pisa Tower was built to hold church bells. No one rings the bells now, as the clanging might make the tower lean faster.

Why was the Eiffel Tower built?

In 1889, a huge international exhibition of art and trade objects was held in Paris, the capital city of France. The Eiffel Tower was built for this exhibition – at that time it was the tallest structure in the world.

? DO YOU KNOW

At just over 646 metres high, the Warszawa radio mast in Poland is the world's tallest structure. It's held up and strengthened by metal cables.

The Eiffel Tower is 300 metres high – taller than 40 two-storey houses! Its strong metal framework is made of iron.

Why was the Statue of Liberty built?

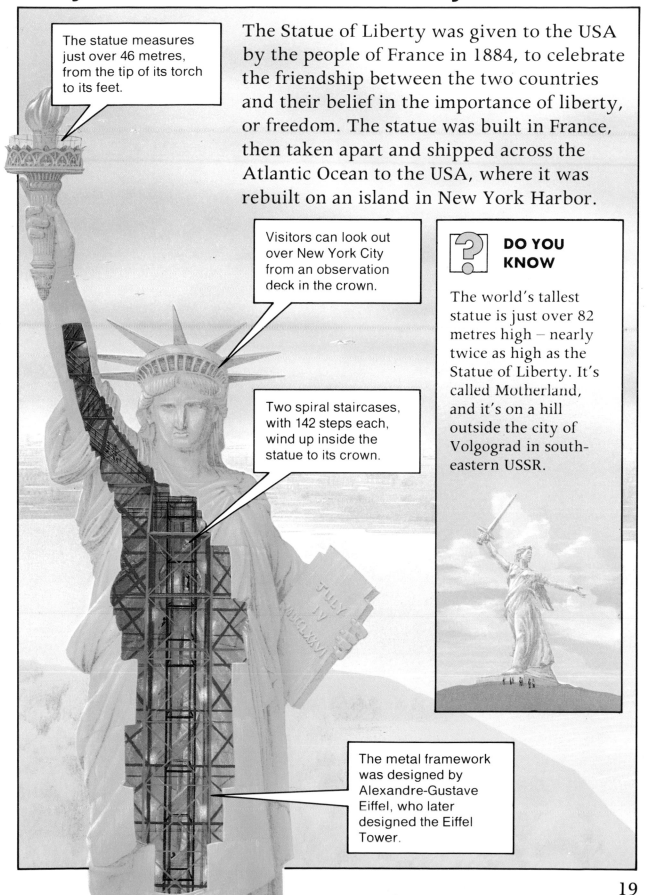

The statue measures just over 46 metres, from the tip of its torch to its feet.

The Statue of Liberty was given to the USA by the people of France in 1884, to celebrate the friendship between the two countries and their belief in the importance of liberty, or freedom. The statue was built in France, then taken apart and shipped across the Atlantic Ocean to the USA, where it was rebuilt on an island in New York Harbor.

Visitors can look out over New York City from an observation deck in the crown.

DO YOU KNOW

The world's tallest statue is just over 82 metres high – nearly twice as high as the Statue of Liberty. It's called Motherland, and it's on a hill outside the city of Volgograd in south-eastern USSR.

Two spiral staircases, with 142 steps each, wind up inside the statue to its crown.

The metal framework was designed by Alexandre-Gustave Eiffel, who later designed the Eiffel Tower.

Why do people build bridges?

Bridges make journeys shorter, easier and safer. They allow us to cross natural barriers such as wide rivers and deep ravines and gorges, for example, and to travel safely over busy roads and railways. Bridges can also be used instead of traffic lights at road junctions, to speed the flow of cars and trucks, and to avoid traffic jams.

? DO YOU KNOW

Not all bridges are made by people. Some are natural rock arches, formed over the centuries by wind or water wearing away soft rock and leaving behind a bridge of harder rock. The Rainbow Bridge in Utah, USA, is a natural rock bridge. Its arch is nearly 90 metres high – a human pyramid of about 50 people could stand under it!

Rainbow Bridge

Footbridges allow people to walk safely over busy roads and railways.

Sometimes bridges are specially built to help farmers get animals and tractors across busy routes.

We wouldn't be able to cross the deep ravines and gorges of mountainous country without bridges.

Bridge crossings are much quicker for people and vehicles than ferry boats are.

Complicated bridge systems like this are built at major road junctions. Traffic lights would slow cars and trucks down.

DO YOU KNOW

The part of a bridge that carries the path, road or railway is called the deck. The supports at each end of a bridge are called abutments. Vertical, or upright, supports are called piers.

The span is the section of a bridge that lies between two supports. The main span is the widest one.

Abutment

Deck

Main span

Abutment

Piers

What types of bridge are there?

There are three basic types of bridge – beam, arch and suspension. The fourth bridge illustrated below, the cantilever, is a type of beam bridge. Beam bridges are very common – you may have made one yourself, by laying a plank or a log across a stream.

1 BEAM BRIDGE

— Piers —

Abutment

2 CANTILEVER BRIDGE

Beam

Cantilever

3 ARCH BRIDGE

Arch

4 SUSPENSION BRIDGE

Main cable

Hanger cables

TEST BRIDGE DESIGN

Find out which is stronger – a beam or an arch bridge. Make both bridges from pieces of stiff paper and books. Pile the same number of wooden blocks in the middle of each bridge – which one collapses first?

BEAM

ARCH

1 Many beam bridges rest on piers as well as abutments.

2 Cantilever bridges are a type of beam bridge. They are made from sections which are supported only at one end. The sections are sometimes linked by a beam.

3 Arch bridges can have more than one arch.

4 The word suspension means hang, and these bridges hang from strong metal ropes called cables.

Can bridges move?

Some river bridges are designed to allow large ships to pass through them. Tower Bridge over the River Thames in London is this type of bridge. Its deck, or roadway, is in two parts, which can be raised high above the river. Bridges like Tower Bridge are called bascules or drawbridges. They were first used over castle moats.

The deck of London's Tower Bridge splits in the middle when it is raised to let big ships pass through.

Machinery inside the tower pulls one end of the deck downwards, raising the other end.

MOVING BRIDGE FACTS

- The deck of some bridges swings sideways, to allow ships to pass on either side.

- On other bridges, the whole deck can be raised straight up between two towers so ships can sail beneath.

How are suspension bridges built?

With their tall slender towers and long main spans, suspension bridges are among the world's most beautiful and impressive structures. Like all bridges, though, they have to be strong enough to carry their own weight, as well as that of the people and vehicles that use them. The weight of a suspension bridge is carried by its two main cables, so these have to be anchored very firmly into the ground.

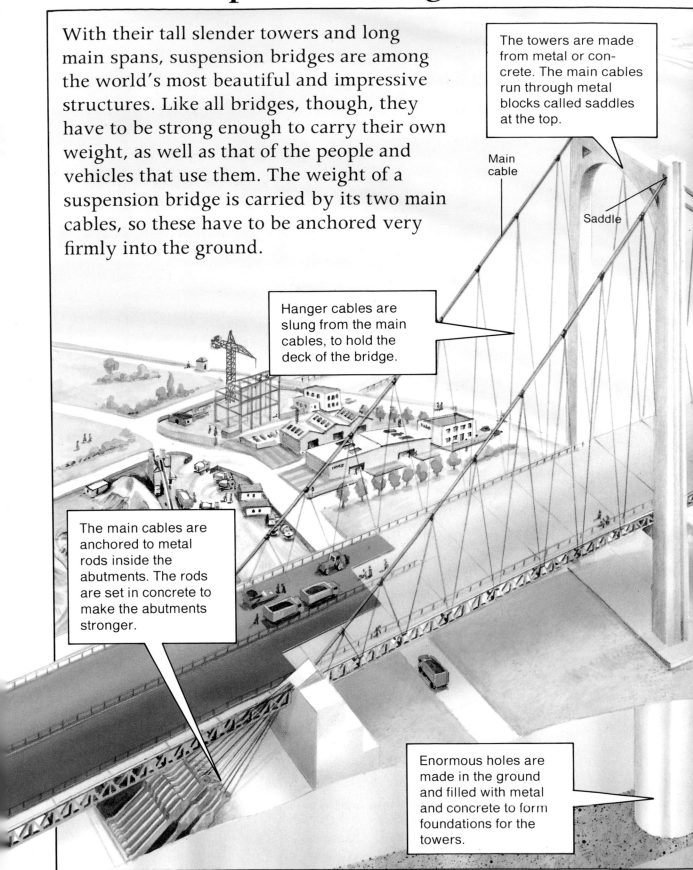

The towers are made from metal or concrete. The main cables run through metal blocks called saddles at the top.

Main cable

Saddle

Hanger cables are slung from the main cables, to hold the deck of the bridge.

The main cables are anchored to metal rods inside the abutments. The rods are set in concrete to make the abutments stronger.

Enormous holes are made in the ground and filled with metal and concrete to form foundations for the towers.

Deck sections are brought to the site on barges which are towed by tugboats.

When all the deck sections are in place, they are welded together. The road is then laid on top.

The deck is built from sections. Each section is hoisted up and fixed to the hanger cables.

? DO YOU KNOW

Foundations for bridge towers and piers are often built in water. One method of building foundations in water is to drive long metal beams into the river or sea bed to make a watertight box called a cofferdam. Water is pumped out of the cofferdam while the foundations are built inside it.

Which are the oldest bridges?

The clapper bridges of south-west England are thought to be the oldest bridges in the world that are still standing, but it isn't possible to date them exactly. The oldest datable bridge was built nearly 3000 years ago, across the River Meles in Turkey.

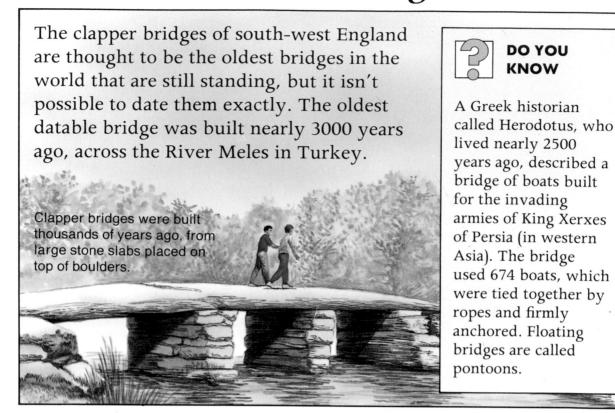

Clapper bridges were built thousands of years ago, from large stone slabs placed on top of boulders.

? DO YOU KNOW

A Greek historian called Herodotus, who lived nearly 2500 years ago, described a bridge of boats built for the invading armies of King Xerxes of Persia (in western Asia). The bridge used 674 boats, which were tied together by ropes and firmly anchored. Floating bridges are called pontoons.

What is an aqueduct?

An aqueduct is a bridge which is specially designed to carry water. The Romans were great bridge builders, and many of their aqueducts are still standing.

The Pont du Gard was built by the Romans nearly 2000 years ago. It is part of an aqueduct system which carried water more than 40 km to supply the city of Nîmes in southern France.

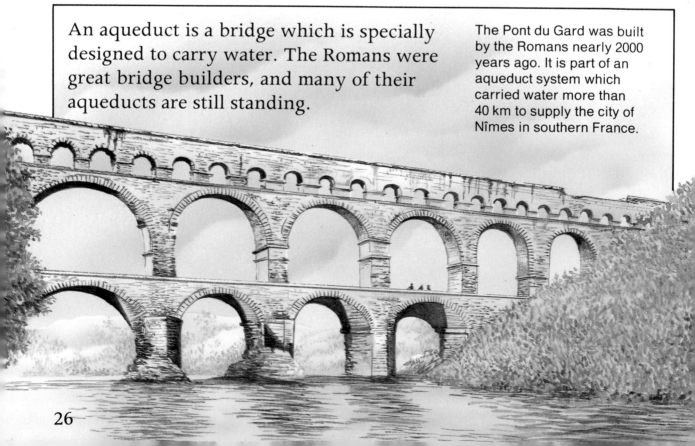

When did people live on bridges?

People were building houses on bridges in European cities about a thousand years ago — shops, churches, and even prisons were built on bridges, too!

The Ponte Vecchio spans the River Arno in Florence, Italy. It was built in the 1300s, and there are still shops and houses on it today.

Where is the Bridge of Sighs?

The Bridge of Sighs is in the northern Italian city of Venice. It was built in the 1590s, to connect the palace of the city's chief judge to the prison. It is named for the sighs of the people who crossed it on their way to prison.

 DO YOU KNOW

The city of Venice is built on about 120 islands. It has canals instead of roads, and more than 400 bridges have been built across its waterways.

Which is the longest bridge?

The world's longest bridging crosses Lake Pontchartrain in Louisiana, USA. There are two causeways, and they're so long that you can't see land from the middle of them – together they measure nearly 77 km!

The bridge with the longest span in the world crosses the River Humber in Yorkshire, northern England. Its main span is 1410 metres long.

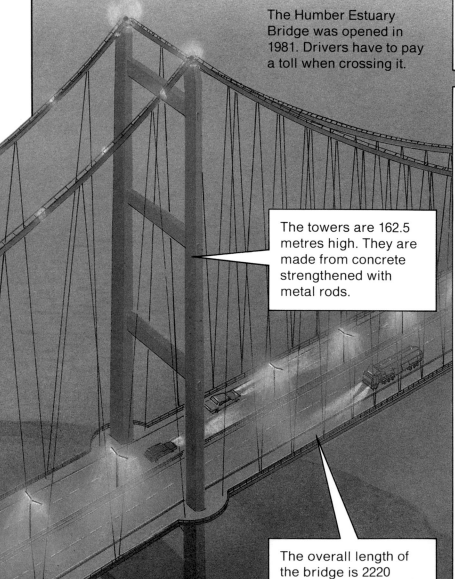

The Humber Estuary Bridge was opened in 1981. Drivers have to pay a toll when crossing it.

The towers are 162.5 metres high. They are made from concrete strengthened with metal rods.

The overall length of the bridge is 2220 metres. Its main span measures 1410 metres.

? DO YOU KNOW

The world's first all-iron bridge was built over the River Severn in the English Midlands in 1779.

BRIDGE OF KNIVES

1 Amaze your friends with this building trick. Challenge them to use three long-bladed table knives and three glasses to build a bridge strong enough to support a fourth glass.

Overlap the knife blades

2 The secret to success lies in the way the knife blades lock together, as the illustration above shows!

Which is the widest bridge?

The Sydney Harbour Bridge is the widest long-span bridge in the world. Its main span measures 49 metres across and is 503 metres long. The bridge is a steel arch and it opened in 1932. Sydney is the capital of the Australian state of New South Wales.

The Sydney Harbour Bridge carries two railway tracks and eight traffic lanes as well as a footpath. It is 49 metres wide.

SYDNEY HARBOUR BRIDGE

Which is the highest bridge?

The highest bridge in the world crosses the Royal Gorge of the Arkansas River in Colorado, USA. This graceful suspension bridge towers 321 metres above the surface of the river – the Eiffel Tower would fit comfortably beneath it!

The Arkansas River Bridge carries road traffic and is the world's highest bridge. It was built in 1929 – in just six months!

Why do people build tunnels?

Like bridges, most tunnels are built to solve travel and transport problems. By burrowing through steep mountains, below wide rivers, and beneath busy city streets, tunnels make it quicker and easier for us to get from one place to another – whether on foot, or in cars or trains.

TEST TUNNEL DESIGN

Most tunnels have arched roofs, because this shape is stronger than a square. Here's a way to compare the strength of arches and squares.

1 You'll need a cardboard tube and a box with a lid. Put them in damp sand. Mold more damp sand firmly around them.

2 Slowly and gently, slide the box and the tube out of the sand. Now press down on the sand above each tunnel until it collapses. Which tunnel caved in first, the arch or the square?

? DO YOU KNOW

The roof of a tunnel is called the crown. Its entrance or mouth is called the portal.

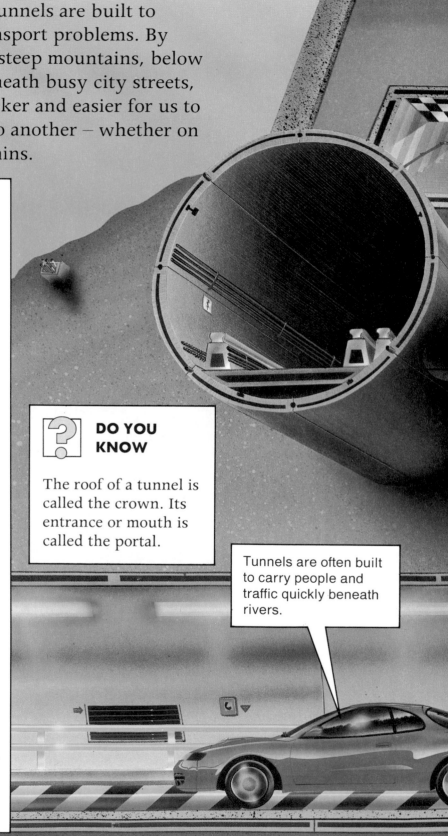

Tunnels are often built to carry people and traffic quickly beneath rivers.

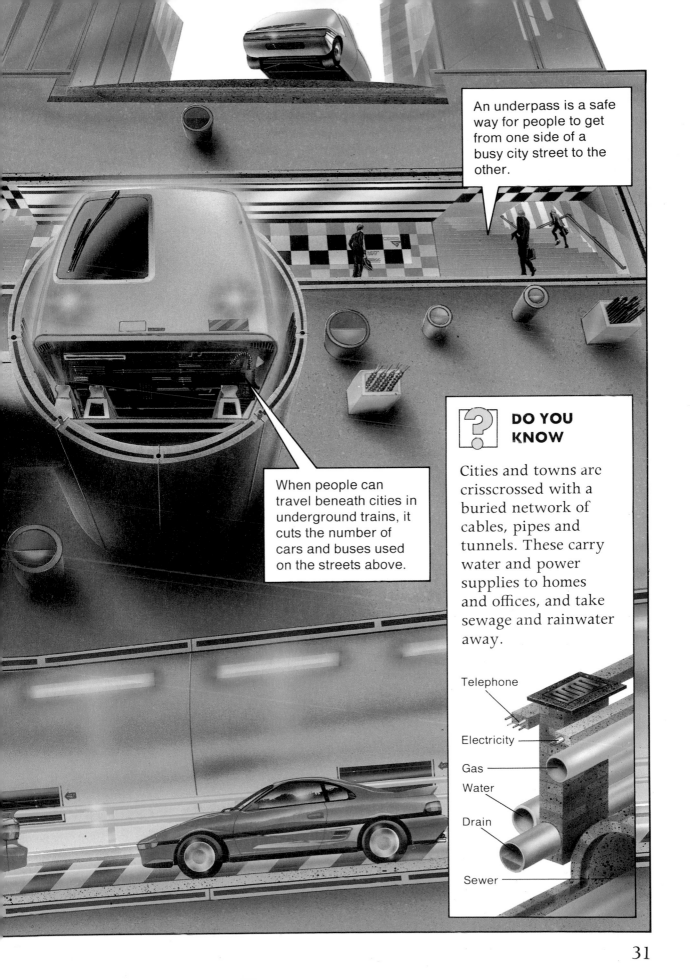

An underpass is a safe way for people to get from one side of a busy city street to the other.

When people can travel beneath cities in underground trains, it cuts the number of cars and buses used on the streets above.

DO YOU KNOW

Cities and towns are crisscrossed with a buried network of cables, pipes and tunnels. These carry water and power supplies to homes and offices, and take sewage and rainwater away.

Telephone
Electricity
Gas
Water
Drain
Sewer

How are tunnels bored?

Before work starts on boring a tunnel, scientists carry out tests to find out what the soil and rock are like along its route. If the scientists discover that the rock is soft and firm – chalk, for example – a tunnel-boring machine (TBM) similar to the one below is used. TBMs are like giant drills, which bore tunnels through rock as they rotate, or turn.

TBM FACTS

● The fastest TBMs can bore tunnels at a rate of more than 120 metres a day.

● The biggest can carve out tunnels 11 metres wide.

A conveyor belt carries away the rock and soil carved out by the TBM head.

Inside the TBM is a long rotating screw which pushes the rock and soil backwards.

The head of the TBM has cutting rollers and teeth. As the head rotates, these eat away at the rock face.

The TBM is pushed forwards by pieces of equipment called hydraulic jacks.

How are tunnels lined?

**AIR
SAFETY**

When fresh air is
pumped into tunnels
for people to breathe,
it helps to get rid of
stale air and the
exhaust fumes from
cars at the same time.
Try this experiment to
see how fresh air can
push out stale air.

1 Seal the ends of a
cardboard tube with
paper and sticky tape.

2 Make two holes in
the tube, and push a
bendy drinking straw
into each one. Seal
any gaps with clay.

3 Angle one straw
towards your cheek.
Now put the other one
in your mouth and
blow – can you feel
'stale' air being
pushed out of the tube
on to your cheek?

When a tunnel is bored through soft rock,
it has to be lined to stop the roof and sides
from collapsing. The linings are made from
huge concrete or metal segments, which are
lifted into position by machines as the TBM
bores its way through the ground.

Gaps between the
tunnel wall and lining
segments are filled
with concrete to seal
the tunnel and make it
watertight.

Lining segments are
big and heavy, so
machines are used to
lift them into place.

When do tunnellers use explosives?

Some types of rock are much harder than others – coal is much harder than chalk, for example. If the route of a tunnel lies through very hard rock, workers blast their way through with explosives such as dynamite. Drills are mounted on a platform called a jumbo and used to make holes in the rock face. Explosives are placed in the holes and then detonated, or set off.

 DRILL FACTS

● When explosives are put in angled holes and detonated, they break up more rock than they would do placed in horizontal, or level, holes.

Angled holes

● Drill holes are usually 2 to 3.5 metres deep and about 6 cm across. Holes this size can be drilled in 4 to 5 minutes.

Jumbos often have several drills. Each one is fitted to the end of a movable boom, or arm.

As they bore into the rock, the drills give off clouds of choking dust. Some jumbos spray water to settle the dust by turning it into mud.

? DO YOU KNOW

The St Gotthard railway tunnel through the Swiss Alps was the first major tunnel to be made using dynamite and a jumbo. It opened in the year 1882.

Some jumbos are mounted on trucks with wheels. Others are set on carriages which run on rails.

What are sunken-tube tunnels?

These are underwater tunnels which are built from huge metal or concrete tubes. The tubes are made in a factory, where they are sealed at both ends. Next they are taken to the tunnel site and towed into position by barges. Then they are lowered into a trench in the river or sea bed.

? DO YOU KNOW

The BART (Bay Area Rapid Transit) underground railway system includes the world's longest and deepest sunken-tube tunnels. Twin tunnels nearly 6 km long are positioned about 40 metres below the surface of San Francisco Bay, on the west coast of the USA.

1 Barges are used to tow the tubes into position and lower them into a trench in the river or sea bed.

2 Divers bolt the outside of the tubes together and seal the joins with concrete. They cover the tubes with sand and mud to protect them.

3 Workers go inside the tubes to cut away the seals at each end. The tubes are then welded together to make one long water-tight tunnel.

? DO YOU KNOW

Cut-and-cover is a method of building land tunnels that don't have to be deep below the ground. Workers simply dig a trench, line it, and cover it up again.

35

Who built the first tunnels?

Tunnelling began many thousands of years ago, when people dug holes to make the caves they lived in bigger. About 15,000 years ago, people started digging tunnels to mine a hard stone called flint for making tools and weapons.

DO YOU KNOW

The Romans built the first-known road tunnel over 2000 years ago, in 36 BC. It was near the city of Naples in southern Italy, and it was nearly 1.5 km long.

About 3500 years ago, after they stopped building pyramids, the Egyptians began making tombs like this by tunnelling into soft rock. The tombs were decorated with beautiful wall-paintings.

Where was the first subway built?

The world's first subway, or underground railway, was built in London and opened in 1863. At that time trains were pulled by steam locomotives. The first electric subway opened in London 27 years later.

SUBWAY FACTS

● The USA's first subway opened in Boston in 1897.

● France's first subway, the Paris Métro, opened in 1900.

● The Moscow Metro, in the USSR, opened in the 1930s. Today it has the world's longest stretch of subway (nearly 31 km long).

Which are the longest tunnels?

The longest traffic tunnel in the world is a railway tunnel, the Seikan Tunnel in Japan. It is almost 54 km long and it links the islands of Hokkaido and Honshu – just over 23 km of the tunnel is under the sea.

? DO YOU KNOW

The world's longest tunnel is in the USA. It runs for 169 km, carrying water from mountain reservoirs to New York City.

ARLBERG Austria (road) 14 km

ST GOTTHARD Switzerland (road) 16 km

SIMPLON II Italy-Switzerland (railway) 20 km

OSHIMIZU Japan (railway) 22 km

SEIKAN Japan (railway) 54 km

Where are the deepest tunnels?

The world's deepest tunnels are more than 3800 metres below the Earth's surface – you could fit the world's tallest building, the Sears Tower, into this depth 8.5 times! The tunnels are part of the Western Deep gold mine in South Africa.

? DO YOU KNOW

The Eisenhower Tunnel in Colorado, USA, is the world's highest (3400 metres above sea level).

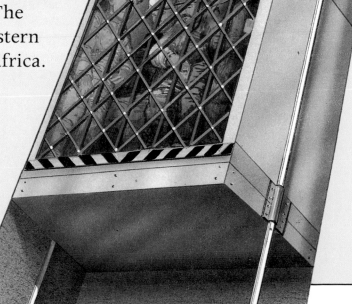

What is the Eurotunnel?

The Eurotunnel is in fact three tunnels (two railway and one service) which are being dug under the sea between Britain and France. When it is completed in the mid-1990s, the Eurotunnel will be nearly 50 km long. It will run below the sea for roughly 37 km, making it the world's longest underwater tunnel.

DO YOU KNOW

The first plans for a tunnel under the Channel were put forward in 1802 by a Frenchman, Albert Mathieu-Favier. People were to travel in horse-drawn carriages along a tunnel lit by candles. The journey would have taken roughly 5 hours.

The two rail tunnels measure just over 7.5 metres across. The service tunnel is nearly 5 metres across.

Workers will travel along the service tunnel to carry out repairs. It will also be used as an escape route in emergencies.

Trains will carry cars and passengers from England to France in around 30 minutes – that's less than half the time the crossing takes by ferry.

BRITAIN

ENGLISH CHANNEL

Dover

Calais

Tunnel route

Folkestone

FRANCE

Useful words

Abutments The supports at each end of a bridge.

Architect Someone who designs buildings and draws up plans for them.

Cable A thick strong rope, often made from several metal wires twisted together.

Cement A building material made by mixing and burning clay and chalk, then grinding them into a fine powder. The powder becomes a paste when mixed with water, and the paste sets hard when it dries.

Concrete A very hard building material made by mixing sand, small stones or crushed rock, cement and water – it sets like rock when it dries.

Deck The surface of a bridge – the part that carries the path, road or railway.

Foundations The strong solid base on which a building or other structure rests. Foundations support the framework and stop heavy structures from sinking into soft ground.

Girder A long straight metal beam. Girders are usually made from steel.

Mortar A building material used in wall-building to stick bricks and stones together. It's made by mixing sand, cement and water into a paste which dries hard. Lime is sometimes added to the paste as well.

Pier A vertical, or upright, support for the span of a bridge.

Reinforced concrete Concrete strengthened with metal rods.

Span The part of a bridge that lies between two supports (abutments, towers or piers). The widest span is called the main span.

Storey One level of a building.

Weld To join two pieces of metal by heating the edges until they melt and mix. A solid join forms when they cool.

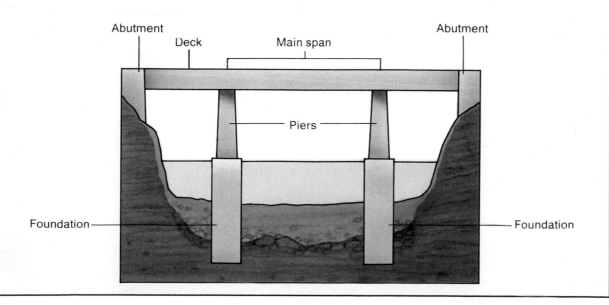

Index